T0247354

FEFU AND HER FRIENDS

NEW, EXPANDED EDITION

MARIA IRENE FORNES

New York, New York

BOOKS BY MARIA IRENE FORNES

Fefu and Her Friends
Maria Irene Fornes: Plays
Promenade and Other Plays
Letters from Cuba
What of the Night?: Selected Plays

Fefu and Her Friends is published by PAJ Publications, P. O. Box 532, Village Station, New York, NY 10014. PAJ Publications is distributed to the trade by Consortium Book Sales and Distribution: www.cbsd.com

Publisher of PAJ Publications: Bonnie Marranca
Full catalogue of PAJ Publications is available from Theatre Communications Group, www.tcg.org

LIBRARY OF CONGRESS CATALOGUING-IN-PUBLICATION DATA

Names: Fornes, Maria Irene, author.
Title: Fefu and her friends / Maria Irene Fornes.
Description: New, expanded edition. | New York : PAJ Publications, [2017]
Identifiers: LCCN 2017010398 | ISBN 9781555541637
Classification: LCC PS3556.O7344 F43 2017 | DDC 812/.54—dc23
LC record available at https://lccn.loc.gov/2017010398

FEFU and HER FRIENDS

Author's Note: Fefu is pronounced Feh-foo.

Fefu and Her Friends was first produced by the New York Theatre Strategy at the Relativity Media Lab, New York City, on May 5, 1977. It was directed by the author. Set design by Linda Conaway. Lights by Candice Dunn. Costumes by Lana Fritz.

Original cast:

Fefu	*Rebecca Schull*
Cindy	*Gwendolyn Brown*
Christina	*Carolyn Hearn*
Julia	*Margaret Harrington*
Emma	*Gordana Rashovich*
Paula	*Connie LoCurto Cicone*
Sue	*Janet Biehl*
Cecilia	*Joan Voukides*

The play was subsequently produced by the American Place Theatre, New York City, on January 8, 1978.

———

New England, Spring 1935.

Part I: Noon. The living room. The entire audience watches from the main auditorium.

Part II: Afternoon. The lawn, the study, the bedroom, the kitchen. The audience is divided into four groups. Each group is led to the spaces. These scenes are performed simultaneously. When the scenes are completed the audience moves to the next space and the scenes are performed again. This is repeated four times until each group has seen all four scenes. Then the audience is led back to the main auditorium.

Part III: Evening. The living room. The entire audience watches from the main auditorium.

Part I

(*The living room of a country house in New England. The decor is a tasteful mixture of styles. To the right is the foyer and the main door. To the left, French doors leading to a terrace, the lawn and a pond. At the rear, there are stairs that lead to the upper floor, the entrance to the kitchen, and the entrance to other rooms on the ground floor. A couch faces the audience. There is a coffee table, two chairs on each side of the table. Upstage right there is a piano. Against the right wall there is an open liquor cabinet. Besides bottles of liquor there are glasses, an ice bucket, and a seltzer bottle. A double barrel shotgun leans on the wall near the French doors. On the table there is a dish with chocolates. On the couch there is a throw. Fefu stands on the landing. Cindy lies on the couch. Christina sits on the chair to the right.*)

FEFU: My husband married me to have a constant reminder of how loathsome women are.

CINDY: What?

FEFU: Yup.

CINDY: That's just awful.

FEFU: No, it isn't.

CINDY: It isn't awful?

FEFU: No.

CINDY: I don't think anyone would marry for that reason.

FEFU: He did.

CINDY: Did he say so?

FEFU: He tells me constantly.

CINDY: Oh, dear.

FEFU: I don't mind. I laugh when he tells me.

CINDY: You laugh?

FEFU: I do.

CINDY: How can you?

FEFU: It's funny.—And it's true. That's why I laugh.

CINDY: What is true?

FEFU: That women are loathsome.

CINDY: . . . Fefu!

FEFU: That shocks you.

CINDY: It does. I don't feel loathsome.

FEFU: I don't mean that you are loathsome.

CINDY: You don't mean that I'm loathsome.

FEFU: No . . . It's something to think about. It's a thought.

CINDY: It's a hideous thought.

FEFU: I take it all back.

CINDY: Isn't she incredible?

FEFU: Cindy, I'm not talking about anyone in particular. It's something to think about.

CINDY: No one in particular, just women.

FEFU: Yes.

CINDY: In that case I am relieved. I thought you were referring to us.

FEFU: (*Affectionately.*) You are being stupid.

CINDY: Stupid and loathsome. (*To Christina.*) Have you ever heard anything so outrageous.

CHRISTINA: I am speechless.

FEFU: Why are you speechless?

CHRISTINA: I think you are outrageous.

FEFU: Don't be offended. I don't take enough care to be tactful. I know I don't. But don't be offended. Cindy is not offended. She pretends to be, but she isn't really. She understands what I mean.

CINDY: I do not.

FEFU: Yes, you do.—I like exciting ideas. They give me energy.

CHRISTINA: And how is women being loathsome an exciting idea?

FEFU: (*With mischief.*) It revolts me.

CHRISTINA: You find revulsion exciting?

FEFU: Don't you?

CHRISTINA: No.

FEFU: I do. It's something to grapple with.—What do you do with revulsion?

CHRISTINA: I avoid anything that's revolting to me.

FEFU: Hmmm. (*To Cindy.*) You too?

CINDY: Yes.

FEFU: Hmm. Have you ever turned a stone over in damp soil?

CHRISTINA: Ahm.

FEFU: And when you turn it there are worms crawling on it?

CHRISTINA: Ahm.

FEFU: And it's damp and full of fungus?

CHRISTINA: Ahm.

FEFU: Were you revolted?

CHRISTINA: Yes.

FEFU: Were you fascinated?

CHRISTINA: I was.

FEFU: There you have it! You too are fascinated with revulsion.

CHRISTINA: Hmm.

FEFU: You see, that which is exposed to the exterior . . . is smooth and dry and clean. That which is not . . . underneath, is slimy and filled with fungus and crawling with worms. It is another life that is parallel to the one we manifest. It's there. The way worms are underneath the stone. If you don't recognize it . . . (*Whispering.*) it eats you. That is my opinion. Well, who is ready for lunch?

CINDY: I'll have some fried worms with lots of pepper.

FEFU: (*To Christina.*) You?

CHRISTINA: I'll have mine in a sandwich with mayonnaise.

FEFU: And to drink?

CHRISTINA: Just some dirty dishwater in a tall glass with ice.

(*Fefu looks at Cindy.*)

CINDY: That sounds fine.

FEFU: I'll go dig them up. (*Fefu walks to the French doors. Beckoning Christina.*) Pst! (*Fefu gets the gun as Christina goes to the French doors.*) You haven't met Phillip. Have you?

CHRISTINA: No.

FEFU: That's him.

CHRISTINA: Which one?

FEFU: (*Aims and shoots.*) That one!

(*Christina and Cindy scream. Fefu smiles proudly. She blows on the mouth of the barrel. She puts down the gun and looks out again.*)

CINDY: Christ, Fefu.

FEFU: There he goes. He's up. It's a game we play. I shoot and he falls. Whenever he hears the blast he falls. No matter where he is, he falls. One time he fell in a puddle of mud and his clothes were a mess. (*She looks out.*) It's not too bad. He's just dusting off some stuff. (*She waves to Phillip and starts to go upstairs.*) He's all right. Look.

CINDY: A drink?

CHRISTINA: Yes.

(*Cindy goes to the liquor cabinet.*)

CINDY: What would you like?

CHRISTINA: Bourbon and soda . . . (*Cindy puts ice and bourbon in a glass. As she starts to squirt the soda . . .*) lots of soda. Just soda. (*Cindy starts with a fresh glass. She starts to squirt soda just as Christina speaks.*) Wait. (*Cindy stops squirting, but not soon enough.*) I'll have an ice cube with a few drops of bourbon. (*Cindy starts with a fresh glass.*)

CINDY: One or two ice cubes?

CHRISTINA: One. Something to suck on.

CINDY: She's unique. There's no one like her.

CHRISTINA: Thank God.

(*Cindy gives the drink to Christina.*)

CINDY: But she is lovely you know. She really is.

CHRISTINA: She's crazy.

CINDY: A little. She has a strange marriage.

CHRISTINA: Strange? It's revolting.—What is he like?

CINDY: He's crazy too. They drive each other crazy. They are not crazy really. They drive each other crazy.

CHRISTINA: Why do they stay together?

CINDY: They love each other.

CHRISTINA: Love?

CINDY: It's love.

CHRISTINA: Who are the other two men?

CINDY: Fefu's younger brother, John. And the gardener. His name is Tom.—The gun is not loaded.

CHRISTINA: How do you know?

CINDY: It's not. Why should it be loaded?

CHRISTINA: It seemed to be loaded a moment ago.

CINDY: That was just a blank.

CHRISTINA: It sounded like a cannon shot.

CINDY: That was just gun powder. There's no bullet in a blank.

CHRISTINA: The blast alone could kill you. One can die of fright, you know.

CINDY: True.

CHRISTINA: My heart is still beating.

CINDY: That's just fright. You're being a scaredy cat.

CHRISTINA: Of course it's just fright. It's fright.

CINDY: I mean, you were just scared. You didn't get hurt.

CHRISTINA: Just scared. I guess I was lucky I didn't get shot.

CINDY: Fefu won't shoot you. She only shoots Phillip.

CHRISTINA: That's nice of her. Put the gun away, I don't like looking at it.

FEFU: (*As she appears on the landing.*) I just fixed the toilet in your bathroom.

CINDY: You did?

FEFU: I did. The water stopper didn't work. It drained. I adjusted it. I'm waiting for the tank to fill up. Make sure it all works.

CHRISTINA: You do your own plumbing?

FEFU: I just had to bend the metal that supports the rubber stopper so it falls right over the hole. What happened was it fell to the side so the water wouldn't stop running into the bowl. (*Fefu sits near Cindy.*) He scared me this time, you know. He looked like he was really hurt.

CINDY: I thought the guns were not loaded.

FEFU: I'm never sure.

CHRISTINA: What?

CINDY: Fefu, what do you mean?

FEFU: He told me one day he'll put real bullets in the guns. He likes to make me nervous. (*There is a moment's silence.*) I have upset you . . . I don't mean to upset you. That's the way we are with each other. We always go to extremes but it's not anything to be upset about.

CHRISTINA: You scare me.

FEFU: That's all right. I scare myself too, sometimes. But there's nothing wrong with being scared . . . it makes you stronger.—It does me.—He won't put real bullets in the guns.—It suits our relationship . . . the game, I mean. If I didn't shoot him with blanks, I might shoot him for real. Do you see the sense of it?

CHRISTINA: I think you're crazy.

FEFU: I'm not. I'm sane.

CHRISTINA: (*Gently.*) You're very stupid.

FEFU: I'm not. I'm very bright.

CHRISTINA: (*Gently.*) You depress me.

FEFU: Don't be depressed. Laugh at me if you don't agree with me. Say I'm ridiculous. I know I'm ridiculous. Come on, laugh. I hate to think I'm depressing to you.

CHRISTINA: All right. I'll laugh.

FEFU: I'll make you a drink.

CHRISTINA: No, I'm just sucking on the ice.

FEFU: Don't you feel well?

CHRISTINA: I'm all right.

FEFU: What are you drinking?

CHRISTINA: Bourbon.

FEFU: (*Getting Christina's glass and going to the liquor cabinet.*) Would you like some more? I'll get you some.

CHRISTINA: Just a drop.

FEFU: (*With great care pours a single drop of bourbon on the ice cube.*) Like that?

CHRISTINA: Yes, thank you.

FEFU: (*Gives Christina the drink and watches her put the cube to her lips.*) That's the cutest thing I've ever seen. It's cold. (*Christina nods.*) You need a stick in the ice, like a popsicle stick. You hold the stick and your fingers won't get cold. I have some sticks. I'll do some for you.

CHRISTINA: Don't trouble yourself.

FEFU: It won't be any trouble. You might want some later.—I'm strange, Christina. But I am fortunate in that I don't mind being strange. It's hard on others sometimes. But not that hard. Is it, Cindy? Those who love me, love me precisely because I am the way I am. (*To Cindy.*) Isn't that so? (*Cindy smiles and nods.*)

CINDY: I would love you even if you weren't the way you are.

FEFU: You wouldn't know it was me if I weren't the way I am.

CINDY: I would still know it was you underneath.

FEFU: (*To Christina.*) You see?—There are some good things about me.—I'm never angry, for example.

CHRISTINA: But you make everyone else angry.

(*Fefu thinks a moment.*)

FEFU: No.

CHRISTINA: You've made me furious.

FEFU: I know. And I might make you angry again. Still I would like it if you liked me.—You think it's unlikely.

CHRISTINA: I don't know.

FEFU: . . . We'll see. (*Fefu goes to the doors. She stands there briefly and speaks reflectively.*) I still like men better than women.—I envy them. I like being like a man. Thinking like a man. Feeling like a man.—They are well together. Women are not. Look at them. They are checking the new grass mower. . . . Out in the fresh air and the sun, while we sit here in the dark. . . . Men have natural strength. Women have to find their strength, and when they do find it, it comes forth with bitterness and it's erratic. . . . Women are restless with each other. They are like live wires . . . either chattering to keep themselves from making contact, or else, if they don't chatter, they avert their eyes . . . like Orpheus . . . as if a god once said "and if they shall recognize each other, the world will be blown apart." They are always eager for the men to arrive. When they do, they can put themselves at rest, tranquilized and in a mild stupor. With the men they feel safe. The danger is gone. That's the closest they can be to feeling wholesome. Men are muscle that cover the raw nerve. They are the insulators. The danger is gone, but the price is the mind and the spirit. . . . High price.—I've never understood it. Why?— What is feared?—Hmm. Well . . .—Do you know? Perhaps the heavens would fall.—Have I offended you again?

CHRISTINA: No. I too have wished for that trust men have for each other. The faith the world puts in them and they in turn put in the world. I know I don't have it.

FEFU: Hmm. Well, I have to see how my toilet is doing. (*Fefu goes to the landing and exits. She puts her head out. She smiles.*) Plumbing is more important than you think.

(*Christina falls off her chair in a mock faint. Cindy goes to her.*)

CINDY: What do you think?

CHRISTINA: Think? I hurt. I'm all shreds inside.

CINDY: Anything I can do?

CHRISTINA: Sing.

(*Cindy sings "Winter Wonderland." Christina harmonizes. There is the sound of a horn. Fefu enters.*)

FEFU: It's Julia. (*To Christina, who is on the floor.*) Are you all right?

CHRISTINA: Yes. (*Fefu exits through the foyer.*) Darn it! (*Christina starts to stand.*)

FEFU: (*Off-stage.*) Julia . . . let me help you.

JULIA: I can manage. I'm much stronger now.

FEFU: There you go.

JULIA: You have my bag.

FEFU: Yes.

(*Julia and Fefu enter. Julia is in a wheelchair.*)

JULIA: Hello Cindy.

CINDY: Hello darling. How are you?

JULIA: I'm very well now. I'm driving now. You must see my car. It's very clever the way they worked it all out. You might want to drive it. It's not hard at all. (*Turning to Christina.*) Christina.

CHRISTINA: Hello Julia.

JULIA: I'm glad to see you.

FEFU: I'll take this to your room. You're down here, if you want to wash up.

(Fefu exits through the upstage exit. Julia follows her.)

CINDY: I can't get used to it.

CHRISTINA: She's better. Isn't she?

CINDY: Not really.

CHRISTINA: Was she actually hit by the bullet?

CINDY: No . . . I was with her.

CHRISTINA: I know.

CINDY: I thought the bullet hit her, but it didn't.—How do you know if a person is hit by a bullet?

CHRISTINA: Cindy . . . there's a wound and . . . there's a bullet.

CINDY: Well, the hunter aimed . . . at the deer. He shot.

CHRISTINA: He?

CINDY: Yes.

CHRISTINA: *(Pointing in the direction of Fefu.)* It wasn't. . . ?

CINDY: Fefu? . . . No. She wasn't even there. She used to hunt but she doesn't hunt any more. She loves animals.

CHRISTINA: Go on.

CINDY: He shot. Julia and the deer fell. The deer was dead . . . dying. Julia was unconscious. She had convulsions . . . like the deer. He died and she didn't. I screamed for help and the hunter came and examined Julia. He said, ''She is not hurt.'' Julia's forehead was bleeding. He said, ''It is a surface wound. I didn't hurt her.'' I know it wasn't he who hurt her. It was someone else. He went for help and Julia started talking. She was delirious.—Apparently there was a spinal nerve injury. She hit her head and she suffered a concussion. She blanks out and that is caused by the blow on the head. It's a scar in the brain. It's called the petit mal.

(Fefu enters.)

CHRISTINA: What was it she said?

CINDY: Hmm? . . .

CHRISTINA: When she was delirious.

CINDY: When she was delirious? That she was persecuted.—That they tortured her. . . . That they had tried her and that the shot was her execution. That she recanted because she wanted to live. . . . That if she talked about it . . . to anyone . . . she would be tortured further and killed. And I have not mentioned this before because . . . I fear for her.

CHRISTINA: It doesn't make any sense, Cindy.

CINDY: It makes sense to me. You heard? (*Fefu goes to Cindy and holds her.*)

FEFU: Who hurt her?

CINDY: I don't know.

FEFU: (*To Christina.*) Did you know her?

CHRISTINA: I met her once years ago.

FEFU: You remember her then as she was. . . . She was afraid of nothing. . . . Have you ever met anyone like that? . . . She knew so much. She was so young and yet she knew so much. . . . How did she learn all that? . . . (*To Cindy.*) Did you ever wonder? Well, I still haven't checked my toilet. Can you believe that. I still haven't checked it. (*Fefu goes upstairs.*)

CHRISTINA: How long ago was the accident?

CINDY: A year . . . a little over a year.

CHRISTINA: Is she in pain?

CINDY: I don't think so.

CHRISTINA: We are made of putty. Aren't we?

(*There is the sound of a car. Car doors opening and closing. A house window opening.*)

FEFU: (*Off-stage.*) Emma! What is that you're wearing. You look marvelous.

EMMA: (*Off-stage.*) I got it in Turkey.

FEFU: Hi Paula, Sue.

PAULA: Hi.

SUE: Hi.

(*Cindy goes out to greet them. Julia enters. She wheels herself to the downstage area.*)

FEFU: I'll be right down! Hey, my toilet works.

EMMA: Stephany. Mine does too.

FEFU: Don't be funny.

EMMA: Come down.

(*Fefu enters as Emma, Sue, and Paula enter. Emma and Fefu embrace.*)

FEFU: How are you?

EMMA: Good . . . good . . . good . . . .(*Still embracing Fefu, Emma sees Julia.*) Julia! (*She runs to Julia and sits on her lap.*)

FEFU: Emma!

JULIA: It's all right.

EMMA: Take me for a ride. (*Julia wheels the chair in a circle. Emma waves as they ride.*) Hi, Cindy, Paula, Sue, Fefu.

JULIA: Do you know Christina?

EMMA: How do you do.

CHRISTINA: How do you do.

EMMA: (*Pointing.*) Sue . . . Paula . . .

SUE: Hello.

PAULA: Hello.

CHRISTINA: Hello.

PAULA: (*To Fefu.*) I liked your talk at Flossie Crit.

FEFU: Oh god, don't remind me. I thought I was awful. Come, I'll show you your rooms. (*She starts to go up.*)

PAULA: I thought you weren't. I found it very stimulating.

EMMA: When was that? . . . What was it on?

FEFU: Aviation.

PAULA: It wasn't on aviation. It was on Voltairine de Cleyre.

JULIA: I wish I had known.

FEFU: It wasn't important.

JULIA: I would have gone, Fefu.

FEFU: Really, it wasn't worth the trouble.

EMMA: Now you'll have to tell Julia and me all about Voltairine de Cleyre.

FEFU: You know all about Voltairine de Cleyre.

EMMA: I don't.

FEFU: I'll tell you at lunch.

EMMA: I had lunch.

JULIA: You can sit and listen while we eat.

EMMA: I will. When do we start our meeting?

FEFU: After lunch. We'll have something to eat and then we'll have our meeting. Who's ready for lunch?

(*The following lines are said almost simultaneously.*)

CINDY: I am.

JULIA: I'm not really hungry.

CHRISTINA: I could eat now.

PAULA: I'm ready.

SUE: I'd rather wait.

EMMA: I'll have coffee.

FEFU: . . . Well . . . we'll take a vote later.

CINDY: What are we doing exactly?

FEFU: About lunch?

CINDY: That too, but I meant the agenda.

SUE: Well, I thought we should first discuss what each of us is going to talk about, so we don't duplicate what someone else is saying, and then we have a review of it, a sort of rehearsal, so we know in what order we should speak and how long it's going to take.

EMMA: We should do a rehearsal in costume. What color should each wear. It matters. Do you know what you're wearing?

PAULA: I haven't thought about it. What color should I wear?

EMMA: Red.

PAULA: Red!

EMMA: Cherry red or white.

SUE: And I?

EMMA: Dark green.

CINDY: The treasurer should wear green.

EMMA: It suits her too.

SUE: And then we'll speak in order of color.

EMMA: Right. Who else wants to know? (*Cindy and Julia raise their hands. To Cindy.*) For you lavender. (*To Julia.*) Purpurra. (*Fefu raises her hand.*) For you, all the gold in Persia.

FEFU: There is no gold in Persia.

EMMA: In Peru. I brought my costume. I'll put it on later.

FEFU: You're not in costume?

EMMA: No. This is just a dress. My costume is . . . dramatic. I won't tell you any more about it. You'll see it.

SUE: I had no idea we were going to do theatre.

EMMA: Life is theatre. Theatre is life. If we're showing what life is, can be, we must do theatre.

SUE: Will I have to act?

EMMA: It's not acting. It's being. It's springing forth with the powers of the spirit. It's breathing.

JULIA: I'll do a dance.

EMMA: I'll stage a dance for you.

JULIA: Sitting?

EMMA: On a settee.

JULIA: I'm game.

EMMA: (*Takes a deep breath and walks through the French doors.*) Phillip! What are you doing?—Hello.—Hello, John.—What? I'm staging a dance for Julia!

FEFU: We'll never see her again.—Come.

(*Fefu, Paula, and Sue go upstairs. Julia goes to the gun, takes it and smells the mouth of the barrel. She looks at Cindy.*)

CINDY: It's a blank.

(*Julia takes the remaining slug out of the gun. She lets it fall on the floor.*)

JULIA: She's hurting herself. (*Julia looks blank and is motionless. Cindy picks up the slug. She notices Julia's condition.*)

CINDY: Julia. (*To Christina.*) She's absent.

CHRISTINA: What do we do?

CINDY: Nothing, she'll be all right in a moment. (*She takes the gun from Julia. Julia comes to.*)

JULIA: It's a blank . . .

CINDY: It is.

JULIA: She's hurting herself. (*Julia lets out a strange whimper. She goes to the coffee table, takes a piece of chocolate, puts it in her mouth and goes toward her room. After she crosses the threshold, she stops.*) I must lie down a while.

CINDY: Call me if you need anything.

JULIA: I will. (*She exits. Cindy tries to put the slug in the rifle. There is the sound of a car, a car door opening, closing.*)

CINDY: Do you know how to do this?

CHRISTINA: Of course not.

(*Cindy succeeds in putting the slug in the gun. Cecilia stands in the threshold of the foyer.*)

CECILIA: I am Cecilia Johnson. Do I have the right place?

CINDY: Yes.

(*Cindy locks the gun. Lights fade all around Cecilia. Only her head is lit. The light fades.*)

Part II

ON THE LAWN

(There is a bench or a tree stump. Fefu and Emma bring boxes of potatoes, carrots, beets, winter squash, and other vegetables from a root cellar and put them in a small wagon. Fefu wears a hat and gardening gloves.)

EMMA: *(Re-enters carrying a box as Fefu exits.)* Do you think about genitals all the time?

FEFU: Genitals? No, I don't think about genitals all the time.

EMMA: *(Starting to exit.)* I do, and it drives me crazy. Each person I see in the street, anywhere at all . . . I keep thinking of their genitals, what they look like, what position they are in. I think it's odd that everyone has them. Don't you?

FEFU: *(Crossing Emma.)* No, I think it'd be odder if they didn't have them.

(Emma laughs. Fefu re-enters.)

EMMA: I mean, people act as if they don't have genitals.

FEFU: How do people with genitals act?

EMMA: I mean, how can business men and women stand in a
room and discuss business without even one reference to their
genitals. I mean everybody has them. They just pretend they
don't.

FEFU: I see. (*Shifting her glance from left to right with a fiendish
look.*) You mean they should do this all the time.

(*Emma laughs.*)

EMMA: No, I don't mean that. Think of it. Don't you think I'm
right?

FEFU: Yes, I think you're right. (*Fefu sits.*) Oh, Emma, Emma-
EmmaEmma.

EMMA: That's m'name.—Well, you see, it's generally believed that
you go to heaven if you are good. If you are bad you go to hell.
That is correct. However, in heaven they don't judge goodness
the way we think. They don't. They have a divine registry of sexual performance. In that registry they mark down every little sexual activity in your life. If your faith is not entirely in it, if you just
perform as an obligation and you don't feel the most profound
devotion, if your spirit, your heart, and your flesh is not religiously delivered to it, you are condemned. They put you down in the
black list and you don't go to heaven. Heaven is populated with
divine lovers. And in hell live the duds.

FEFU: That's probably true.

EMMA: I knew you'd see it that way.

FEFU: Oh, I do. I do. You see, on earth we are judged by public acts,
and sex is a private act. The partner cannot be said to be the
public, since both partners are engaged. So naturally, it stands to
reason that it's angels who judge our sexual life.

EMMA: Naturally.

(*Pause.*)

FEFU: You always bring joy to me.

EMMA: Thank you.

FEFU: I thank you. (*Fefu becomes distressed. She sits.*) I am in constant pain. I don't want to give in to it. If I do I am afraid I will never recover. . . . It's not physical, and it's not sorrow. It's very strange Emma, I can't describe it, and it's very frightening. . . . It is as if normally there is a lubricant . . . not in the body . . . a spiritual lubricant . . . it's hard to describe . . . and without it, life is a nightmare, and everything is distorted.—A black cat started coming to my kitchen. He's awfully mangled and big. He is missing an eye and his skin is diseased. At first I was repelled by him, but then, I thought, this is a monster that has been sent to me and I must feed him. And I fed him. One day he came and shat all over my kitchen. Foul diarrhea. He still comes and I still feed him.—I am afraid of him. (*Emma kisses Fefu.*) How about a little lemonade?

EMMA: Yes.

FEFU: How about a game of croquet?

EMMA: Fine.

(*Fefu exits. Emma improvises an effigy of Fefu. She puts Fefu's hat and gloves on it.*)

> Not from the stars do I my judgment pluck.
> And yet methinks I have astronomy;
> But not to tell of good or evil luck,
> Of plagues, of dearths, or seasons' quality;
> Nor can I fortune to brief minutes tell,
> Pointing to each his thunder, rain, and wind,
> Or say with princes if it shall go well
> By oft predict that I in heaven find.
> But from thine eyes my knowledge I derive.
> And, constant stars, in them I read such art
> As truth and beauty shall together thrive
> If from thyself to store thou wouldst convert:
>   Or else of thee this I prognosticate,
>   Thy end is truth's and beauty's doom and date.

(If Fefu's entrance is delayed, Emma will sing a popular song of the period. Fefu re-enters with a pitcher and two glasses.)

IN THE STUDY

(There are books on the walls, a desk, Victorian chairs, a rug on the floor. Christina sits behind the desk. She reads a French text book. She mumbles French sentences. Cindy sits to the left of the desk with her feet up on a chair. She looks at a magazine. A few moments pass.)

CHRISTINA: *(Practicing.)* Etes-vous externe ou demi-pensionnaire? La cuisine de votre cantine est-elle bonne, passable ou mauvaise? *(She continues reading almost inaudibly. A moment passes.)*

CINDY: *(Reading.)* A lady in Africa divorced her husband because he was a cheetah.

CHRISTINA: Oh, dear. *(They laugh. They go back to their reading. A moment passes.)* Est-ce que votre professeur interroge souvant les eleves? *(They go back to their reading. A moment passes.)*

CINDY: I suppose . . . when a person is swept off their feet . . . the feet remain and the person goes off . . . with the broom.

CHRISTINA: No . . . when a person is swept off their feet . . . there is no broom.

CINDY: What does the sweeping?

CHRISTINA: An emotion . . . a feeling.

CINDY: Then emotions have bristles?

CHRISTINA: Yes.

CINDY: Now I understand. Do the feet remain?

CHRISTINA: No, the feet fly also . . . but separate from the body. At the end of the leap, just before the landing, they join the ankles and one is complete again.

CINDY: Oh, that sounds nice.

CHRISTINA: It is. Being swept off your feet is nice. Anything else?

CINDY: Not for now. (*They go back to their reading. A moment passes.*) Are you having a good time?

CHRISTINA: Yes, I'm very glad I came.

CINDY: Do you like everybody?

CHRISTINA: Yes.

CINDY: Do you like Fefu?

CHRISTINA: I do . . . She confuses me a little.—I try to be honest . . . and I wonder if she is . . . I don't mean that she doesn't tell the truth. I know she does. I mean a kind of integrity. I know she has integrity too. . . . But I don't know if she's careful with life . . . something bigger than the self . . . I suppose I don't mean with life but more with convention. I think she is an adventurer in a way. Her mind is adventurous. I don't know if there is dishonesty in that. But in adventure there is taking chances and risks, and then one has to, somehow, have less regard or respect for things as they are. That is, regard for a kind of convention, I suppose. I am probably ultimately a conformist, I think. And I suppose I do hold back for fear of being disrespectful or destroying something —and I admire those who are not. But I also feel they are dangerous to me. I don't think they are dangerous to the world; they are more useful than I am, more important, but I feel some of my life is endangered by their way of thinking. Do you understand?

CINDY: Yes, I do.

CHRISTINA: I guess I am proud and I don't like thinking that I am thoughtful of things that have no value.—I like her.

CINDY: I had a terrible dream last night.

CHRISTINA: What was it?

CINDY: I was at a dance. And there was a young doctor I had seen in connection with my health. We all danced in a circle and he identified himself and said that he had spoken to Mike about me, but that it was all right, that he had put it so that it was all right. I was puzzled as to why Mike would mind and why he had spoken to him. Then, suddenly everybody sat down on the floor and pretended they were having singing lessons and one person was practicing Italian. The singing professor was being tested by two secret policemen. They were having him correct the voice of someone they had brought. He apparently didn't know how to do it. Then, one of the policemen put his hands on his vocal cords and kicked him out the door. Then he grabbed me and felt my throat from behind with his thumbs while he rubbed my nipples with his pinkies. Then, he pushed me out the door. Then, the young doctor started cursing me. His mouth moved like the mouth of a horse. I was on an upper level with a railing and I said to him, ''Stop and listen to me.'' I said it so strongly that he stopped. Everybody turned to me in admiration because I had made him stop. Then, I said to him, ''Restrain yourself.'' I wanted to say respect me. I wasn't sure whether the words coming out of my mouth were what I wanted to say. I turned to ask my sister. The young man was bending over and trembling in mad rage. Another man told me to run before the young man tried to kill me. Meg and I ran downstairs. She asked me if I wanted to go to her place. We grabbed a taxi, but before the taxi got enough speed he came out and ran to the taxi and was on the verge of opening the door when I woke up.

(*The door opens. Fefu looks in. Her entrance may interrupt Cindy's speech at any point according to how long it takes her to reach the kitchen.*)

FEFU: Who's for a game of croquet?

CINDY: In a little while.

FEFU: See you outside.

CHRISTINA: That was quite a dream.

CINDY: What do you think it means?

CHRISTINA: I think it means you should go to a different doctor.

CINDY: He's not my doctor. I never saw him before.

CHRISTINA: Well good. I'm sure he's not a good doctor.

(*At the end of the fourth repeat, when Fefu invites them for croquet, Cindy says, ''Oh let's play croquet'' and they follow Fefu.*)

IN THE BEDROOM

(*A plain unpainted room. Perhaps a room that was used for storage and was set up as a sleeping place for Julia. There is a mattress on the floor. To the right of the mattress there is a small table, to the left is Julia's wheelchair. There is a sink on the wall. There are dry leaves on the floor although the time is not fall. The sheets are linen. Julia lies in bed covered to her shoulders. She wears a white hospital gown. Julia hallucinates. However, her behavior should not be the usual behavior attributed to a mad person. It should be rather still and luminous. There will be aspects of her hallucination that frighten her, but hallucinating itself does not.*)

JULIA: They clubbed me. They broke my head. They broke my will. They broke my hands. They tore my eyes out. They took my voice away. They didn't do anything to my heart because I didn't bring my heart with me. They clubbed me again, but my head did not fall off in pieces. That was because they were so good and they felt sorry for me. The judges. You didn't know the judges?—I was good and quiet. I never dropped my smile. I smiled to everyone. If I stopped smiling I would get clubbed because they love me. They say they love me. I go along with that because if I don't . . .

(*With her finger she indicates her throat being cut and makes the sound that usually accompanies that gesture.*)

I told them the stinking parts of the body are the important ones: the genitals, the anus, the mouth, the armpit. All important parts except the armpits. And who knows, maybe the armpits are important too. That's what I said. (*Her voice becomes gravelly and tight in imitation of the judges.*) He said that all those parts must be kept clean and put away. He said that women's entrails are heavier than anything on earth and to see a woman running creates a disparate and incongruous image in the mind. It's anti-aesthetic. Therefore women should not run. Instead they should strike positions that take into account the weight of their entrails. Only if they do, can they be aesthetic. He said, for example, Goya's Maja. He said Ruben's women are not aesthetic. Flesh. He said that a woman's bottom should be in a cushion, otherwise it's revolting. He said there are exceptions. Ballet dancers are exceptions. They can run and lift their legs because they have no entrails. Isadora Duncan had entrails, that's why she should not have danced. But she danced and for this reason became crazy. (*Her voice is back to normal.*) She wasn't crazy.

(*She moves her hand as if guarding from a blow.*)

She was. He said that I had to be punished because I was getting too smart. I'm not smart. I never was. Neither is Fefu smart. They are after her too. Well, she's still walking!

(*She guards from a blow. Her eyes close.*)

Wait! I'll say my prayers. I'm saying it.

(*She mumbles. She opens her eyes with caution.*)

You don't think I'm going to argue with them, do you? I repented. I told them exactly what they wanted to hear. They killed me. I was dead. The bullet didn't hit me. It hit the deer. But I died. He didn't. Then I repented and the deer died and I lived. (*With a gravelly voice.*) They said, ''Live but crippled. And if you tell . . .''

(*She repeats the throat cutting gesture.*)

Why do you have to kill Fefu, for she's only a joker? (*With a gravelly voice.*) ''Not kill, cure. Cure her.'' Will it hurt?

(*She whimpers.*)

Oh, dear, dear, my dear, they want your light. Your light my dear. Your precious light. Oh dear, my dear.

(*Her head moves as if slapped.*)

Not cry. I'll say my prayer. I'll say it. Right now. Look.

(She sits up as if pulled by an invisible force.)

The human being is of the masculine gender. The human being is a boy as a child and grown up he is a man. Everything on earth is for the human being, which is man. To nourish him.—There are evil things on earth, and noxious things. Evil and noxious things are on earth for man also. For him to fight with, and conquer and turn its evil into good. So that it too can nourish him.—There are Evil Plants, Evil Animals, Evil Minerals, and Women are Evil.—Woman is not a human being. She is: 1—A mystery. 2—Another species. 3—As yet undefined. 4—Unpredictable; therefore wicked and gentle and evil and good which is evil.—If a man commits an evil act, he must be pitied. The evil comes from outside him, through him and into the act. Woman generates the evil herself.—God gave man no other mate but woman. The oxen is good but it is not a mate for man. The sheep is good but it is not a mate for man. The mate for man is woman and that is the cross man must bear.—Man is not spiritually sexual, he therefore can enjoy sexuality. His sexuality is physical which means his spirit is pure. Women's spirit is sexual. That is why after coitus they dwell in nefarious feelings. Because that is their natural habitat. That is why it is difficult for them to return to the human world. Their sexual feelings remain with them till they die. And they take those feelings with them to the afterlife where they corrupt the heavens, and they are sent to hell where through suffering they may shed those feelings and return to earth as man.

(Her head moves as if slapped.)

Don't hit me. Didn't I just say my prayer?

(A smaller slap.)

I believe it.

(She lies back.)

They say when I believe the prayer I will forget the judges. And when I forget the judges I will believe the prayer. They say both happen at once. And all women have done it. Why can't I?

(Sue enters with a bowl of soup on a tray.)

SUE: Julia, are you asleep?

(*Short pause.*)

JULIA: No.

SUE: I brought your soup.

JULIA: Put it down. I'm getting up in a moment.

(*Sue puts the soup down.*)

SUE: Do you want me to help you?

JULIA: No, I can manage. Thank you, Sue.

(*Sue goes to the door.*)

SUE: You're all right?

JULIA: Yes.

SUE: I'll see you later.

JULIA: Thank you, Sue.

(*Sue exits. Julia closes her eyes. As soon as each audience group leaves, the tray is removed, if possible through a back door.*)

IN THE KITCHEN

(*A fully equipped kitchen. There is a table and chairs and a high cutting table. On a counter next to the stove there is a tray with a soup dish and a spoon. There is also a ladle. On the cutting table there are two empty glasses. Soup is heating on a burner. A kettle with water sits on an unlit burner. In the refrigerator there is an ice tray with wooden sticks in each cube. The sticks should rest on the edge of the tray forming two parallel rows, like a caterpillar lying on its back. In the refrigerator there are also two pitchers, one with water, one with lemonade. Paula sits at the table. She is writing on a pad. Sue waits for the soup to heat.*)

PAULA: I have it all figured out.

SUE: What?

PAULA: A love affair lasts seven years and three months.

SUE: It does?

PAULA: (*Reading.*) 3 months of love. 1 year saying: It's all right. This is just a passing disturbance. 1 year trying to understand what's wrong. 2 years knowing the end had come. 1 year finding the way to end it. After the separation, 2 years trying to understand what happened. 7 years, 3 months. (*No longer reading.*) At any point the sequence might be interrupted by another love affair that has the same sequence. That is, it's not really interrupted, the new love affair relegates the first one to a second plane and both continue their sequence at the same time.

(*Sue looks over Paula's shoulder.*)

SUE: You really added it up.

PAULA: Sure.

SUE: What do you want to drink?

PAULA: Water. The old love affair may fade, so you are not aware the process goes on. A year later it may surface and you might find yourself figuring out what's wrong with the new one while trying to end the old one.

SUE: So how do you solve the problem?

PAULA: Celibacy?

SUE: (*Going to the refrigerator.*) Celibacy doesn't solve anything.

PAULA: That's true.

SUE: (*Taking out the ice tray with the sticks.*) What's this? (*Paula shakes her head.*) Dessert. (*Paula shrugs her shoulders. Sue takes an ice cube and places it against her forehead.*) For a headache.

(*She takes another cube and moves her arms in a Judo style.*) Eskimo wrestling. (*She places one stick behind her ear.*) Brain cooler. That's when you're thinking too much. You could use one. (*She tries to put the ice cube behind Paula's ear. They wrestle and laugh. She puts the stick in her own mouth. She takes it out to speak.*) This is when you want to keep chaste. No one will kiss you. (*She puts it back in to demonstrate. Then takes it out.*) That's good for celibacy. If you walk around with one of these in your mouth for seven years you can keep all your sequences straight. Finish one before you start the other. (*She puts the ice cube in the tray and looks at it.*) A frozen caterpillar. (*She puts the tray away.*)

PAULA: You're leaving that ice cube in there?

SUE: I'm clean. (*Looking at the soup.*) So what else do you have on love? (*Sue places a bowl and spoon on the table and sits as she waits for the soup to heat.*)

PAULA: Well, the break-up takes place in parts. The brain, the heart, the body, mutual things, shared things. The mind leaves but the heart is still there. The heart has left but the body wants to stay. The body leaves but the things are still at the apartment. You must come back. You move everything out of the apartment but the mind stays behind. Memory lingers in the place. Seven years later, perhaps seven years later, it doesn't matter any more. Perhaps it takes longer. Perhaps it never ends.

SUE: It depends.

PAULA: Yup. It depends.

SUE: (*Pouring soup in the bowl.*) Something's bothering you.

PAULA: No.

SUE: (*Taking the tray.*) I'm going to take this to Julia.

PAULA: Go ahead.

(*As Sue exits, Cecilia enters.*)

CECILIA: May I come in?

PAULA: Yes . . . Would you like something to eat?

CECILIA: No, I ate lunch.

PAULA: I didn't eat lunch. I wasn't very hungry.

CECILIA: I know.

PAULA: Would you like some coffee?

CECILIA: I'll have tea.

PAULA: I'll make some.

CECILIA: No, you sit. I'll make it. (*Cecilia looks for tea.*)

PAULA: Here it is. (*She gets the tea and gives it to Cecilia.*)

CECILIA: (*As she lights the burner.*) I've been meaning to call you.

PAULA: It doesn't matter. I know you're busy.

CECILIA: Still I would have called you but I really didn't find the time.

PAULA: Don't worry.

CECILIA: I wanted to see you again. I want to see you often.

PAULA: There's no hurry. Now we know we can see each other.

CECILIA: Yes, I'm glad we can.

PAULA: I have thought a great deal about my life since I saw you. I have questioned my life. I can't help doing that. It's been many years and I wondered how you see me now.

CECILIA: You're the same.

PAULA: I felt small in your presence . . . I haven't done all that I could have. All I wanted to do. Our lives have gone in such different directions I cannot help but review what those years have been for me. I gave up, almost gave up. I have missed you in my life. . . . I became lazy. I lost the drive. You abandoned me and I kept going. But after a while I didn't know how to. I didn't know how to go on. I knew why when I was with you. To give you pleasure. So we could laugh together. So we could rejoice together. To bring beauty to the world. . . . Now we look at each other like strangers. We are guarded. I speak and you don't understand my words. I remember every day.

(*Fefu enters. She takes the lemonade pitcher from the refrigerator and two glasses from the top of the refrigerator.*)

FEFU: Emma and I are going to play croquet. You want to join us? . . . No. You're having a serious conversation.

PAULA: Very serious. (*Paula smiles at Cecilia in a conciliatory manner.*) Too serious.

FEFU: (*As she exits.*) Come.

PAULA: I'm sorry. Let's go play croquet.—I'm not reproaching you.

CECILIA: (*Reaching for Paula's hand.*) I know. I've missed you too.

(*They exit. As soon as the audience leaves the props are reset.*)

Part III

(The living room. It is dusk. As the audience enters, two or three of the women are around the piano playing and singing Schubert's "Who Is Silvia." They exit. Emma enters, checks the lights in the room on her hand, looks around the room and goes upstairs. The rest enter through the rear. Cecilia enters speaking.)

CECILIA: Well, we each have our own system of receiving information, placing it, responding to it. *(She sits in the center of the couch; the rest sit around her.)* That system can function with such a bias that it could take any situation and translate it into one formula. That is, I think, the main reason for stupidity or even madness, not being able to tell the difference between things.

SUE: Like?

CECILIA: Like . . . this person is screaming at me. He's a bully. I don't like being screamed at. Another person or the same person screams in a different situation. But you know you have done something that provokes him to scream. He has a good reason. They are two different things, the screaming of one and the screaming of the other. Often that distinction is not made. We cannot survive in a vacuum. We must be part of a community, perhaps 10, 100, 1000. It depends on how strong you are. But even the strongest will need a dozen, three, even one who sees, thinks, and feels as he does. The greater the need for that kind of reassurance, the greater the number that he needs to identify with. Some need to identify with the whole nation. Then, the greater the number the more limited the number of responses and thoughts. A common denominator must be reached. Thoughts, emotions that fit all, have to be limited to a small number. That is, I feel, the concern of the educator—to teach how to be sensitive to the differences in ourselves as well as outside ourselves, not to supervise the memorization of facts. (*Emma's head appears in the doorway to the stairs.*) Otherwise the unusual in us will perish. As we grow we feel we are strange and fear any thought that is not shared with everyone.

JULIA: As I feel I am perishing. My hallucinations are madness, of course, but I wish I could be with others who hallucinate also. I would still know I am mad but I would not feel so isolated.— Hallucinations are real, you know. They are not like dreams. They are as real as all of you here. I have actually asked to be hospitalized so I could be with other nuts. But the doctors don't want to. They can't diagnose me. That makes me even more isolated. (*There is a moment's silence.*) You see, right now, it's an awful moment because you don't know what to say or do. If I were with other people who hallucinate, they would say, "Oh yeah. Sure. It's awful. Those dummies, they don't see anything." (*The others begin to relax.*) It's not so bad, really. I can laugh at it. . . . Emma is ready. We should start. (*The others are hesitant. Julia speaks to Fefu.*) Come on.

FEFU: Sure. (*Fefu begins to move the table. Others help move the table and enough furniture to clear a space in the center. They sit in a semicircle downstage on the floor facing upstage. Cecilia sits on a chair to the left of the semicircle.*) All right. I start. Right?

CINDY: Right.

(*Fefu goes to center and faces the others. Emma sits on the steps. Only her head and legs are visible.*)

FEFU: I talk about the stifling conditions of primary school education, etc. . . . etc. . . . The project . . . I know what I'm going to say but I don't want to bore you with it. We all know it by heart. Blah blah blah blah. And so on and so on. And so on and so on. Then I introduce Emma . . . And now Miss Emma Blake. (*They applaud. Emma shakes her head.*) What.

EMMA: Paula goes next.

FEFU: Does it matter?

EMMA: Of course it matters. Dra-ma-tics. It has to build. I'm in costume.

FEFU: Oh. And now, ladies and gentlemen, Miss Paula Cori will speak on Art as a Tool for Learning. And I tell them the work you have done at the Institute, community centers, essays, etc. Miss Paula Cori.

(*They applaud. Paula goes to center.*)

PAULA: Ladies and gentlemen, I, like my fellow educator and colleague, Stephany Beckmann . . .

FEFU: I am not an educator.

PAULA: What are you?

FEFU: . . . a do gooder, a girl scout.

PAULA: Well, I, like my fellow girl scout Stephany Beckmann say blah blah blah blah, blah blah blah blah and I offer the jewels of my wisdom and experience, which I will write down and memorize, otherwise I would just stand there and stammer and go blank. And even after I memorize it I'm sure I will just stand there and stammer and go blank.

EMMA: I'll work with you on it.

PAULA: However, after our other colleague Miss Emma Blake works with me on it . . . (*In imitation of Emma she brings her hands together and opens her arms as she moves her head back and speaks.*) My impulses will burst forth through a symphony of eloquence.

EMMA: Breathe . . . in . . . (*Paula inhales slowly.*) And bow. (*Paula bows. They applaud.*)

PAULA: (*Coming up from the bow.*) Oh, I liked that. (*She sits.*)

EMMA: Good . . .

(*They applaud.*)

FEFU: And now, ladies and gentlemen, the one and only, the incomparable, our precious, dear Emma Blake.

(*Emma walks to center. She wears a robe which hangs from her arms to the floor.*)

EMMA: From the prologue to ''The Science of Educational Dramatics'' by Emma Sheridan Fry.* (*She takes a dramatic pose and starts. The whole speech is dramatized by interpretive gestures and movements that cover the stage area.*)

Environment knocks at the gateway of the senses. A rain of summons beats upon us day and night. . . . We do not answer. Everything around us shouts against our deafness, struggles with our unwillingness, batters our walls, flashes into our blindness, strives to sieve through us at every pore, begging, fighting, insisting. It shouts, ''Where are you? Where are you?'' But we are deaf. The signals do not reach us.

Society restricts us, school straight jackets us, civilization submerges us, privation wrings us, luxury feather-beds us. The Divine Urge is checked. The Winged Horse balks on the road, and we, discouraged, defeated, dismount and burrow into ourselves. The gates are closed and Divine Urge is imprisoned at Center. Thus we are taken by indifference that is death.

---

*Emma Sheridan Fry taught acting to children at The Educational Alliance in New York from 1903 to 1909. In 1917, her book *Educational Dramatics* was published by Lloyd Adams Noble. The text of Emma's speech is taken from the prologue.

Environment finding the gates closed tries to break in. Turned away, it comes another way. Kept back, it stretches its hands to us. Always scheming to reach us. Never was suitor more insistent than Environment, seeking admission, claiming recognition, signaling to be seen, shouting to be heard. And through the ages we sit inside ourselves deaf, dumb and blind, and will not stir. . . .

. . . Maybe you are not deaf. . . . Perhaps signals reach you. Maybe you stir. . . . The gates give. . . . Eternal Urge pushes through the stupor of our senses, making paths to meet the challenging suitor, windows through which to see him, ears through which to hear him. Environment shouting, "Where are you?" and Center battering at the inner side of the wall crying, "Here I am," and dragging down bars, wrenching gates, prying at port-holes. Listening at cracks, reaching everywhere, and demanding that sense gates be flung open. The gates are open! Eternal Urge stands at the threshold signaling with venturous flag. An imperious instinct lets us know that "all" is ours, and that whatever anyone has ever known, or may ever have or know, we will call and claim. A sense of life universal surges through our life individual. We attack the feast of this table with an insatiable appetite that cries for all.

What are we? A creation of God's consciousness coming now slowly and painfully into recognition of ourselves.

What is Personality? A small part of us. The whole of us is behind that hungry rush at the gates of Senses.

What is Civilization? A circumscribed order in which the whole has not entered.

What is Environment? Our mate, our true mate that clamors for our reunion.

We will meet him. We will seize all, learn all, know all here, that we may fare further on the great quest! The task of Now is only a step toward the task of the Whole! Let us then seek the laws governing real life forces, that coming into their own, they may create, develop and reconstruct. Let us awaken life dormant! Let us, boldly, seizing the star of our intent, lift it as the lantern of our necessity, and let it shine over the darkness of our compliance. Come! The light shines. Come! It brightens our way. Come! Don't let its glorious light pass you by! Come! The day has come!

(Emma throws herself on the couch. Paula embraces her.) Oh, it's so beautiful.

JULIA: It is, Emma. It is.

(They applaud.)

CINDY: Encore! Encore!

(Emma stands.)

EMMA: Environment knocks at the gateway . . . *(She laughs and joins the others in the semi-circle. Paula remains seated on the couch.)* What's next.

FEFU: *(Going center.)* I introduce Cecilia. I don't think I should introduce Cecilia. She should just come after Emma. Now things don't need introduction. *(Imitating Emma as she goes to her seat.)* They are happening.

EMMA: Right!

(Cecilia goes to center.)

CECILIA: Well, as we say in the business, that's a very hard act to follow.

EMMA: Not *very* hard. It's a hard act to follow.

CECILIA: Right. I should say my name first.

FEFU: Yes.

CECILIA: I should breathe too. *(She takes a breath. All except Paula start singing ''Cecilia.'' Cecilia is perplexed and walks backwards till she sits on the couch. She is next to Paula. Unaware of who she is next to, she puts her hand on Paula's leg. At the end of the song Cecilia realizes she is next to Paula and stands.*) I should go before Emma. I don't think anyone should speak after Emma.

CINDY: Right. It should be Fefu, Paula, Cecilia, then Emma, and then Sue explaining the finances and asking for pledges. And the money should roll in. It's very good. (*They applaud.*) Sue . . . (*Sue goes to center.*)

SUE: Yes, blahblahblahblah, pledges and money. (*She does a few balletic moves and bows. They applaud.*)

FEFU: (*As Sue returns to her seat.*) Who's ready for coffee?

CINDY: (*As she stands.*) And dishes.

CHRISTINA: (*As she stands.*) I'll help.

EMMA: (*As she stands.*) Me too.

FEFU: Don't all come. Sit. Sit. You have done enough, relax.

(*They put the furniture back as Emma and Sue jump over the couch making loud warlike sounds. As they exit to the kitchen, Sue tries to get ahead of Emma. Emma speeds ahead of her. All except Julia jump over the couch. All except Cindy and Julia exit.*)

JULIA: I should go do the dishes. I haven't done anything.

CINDY: You can do them tomorrow.

JULIA: True.—So how have you been?

CINDY: Hmm.

JULIA: Let me see. I can tell by looking at your face. Not so bad.

CINDY: Not so bad.

(*There is the sound of laughter from the kitchen. Christina runs in.*)

CHRISTINA: They're having a water fight over who's going to do the dishes.

CINDY: Emma?

CHRISTINA: And Paula, and Sue, all of them. Fefu was getting into it when I left. Cecilia got out the back door.

(*Christina walks back to the kitchen with some caution. She runs back and lies on the couch covering her head with the throw. Emma enters with a pan of water in her hand. She is wet. Cindy and Julia point to the lawn. Emma runs to the lawn. There is the sound of knocking from upstairs. While the following conversation goes on, Emma, Sue, Cindy, and Julia engage in water fights in and out of the living room. The screams, laughter, and water splashing may drown the words.*)

PAULA: Open up.

FEFU: There's no one here.

PAULA: Open up you coward.

FEFU: I can't. I'm busy.

PAULA: What are you doing?

FEFU: I have a man here. Ah ah ah ah ah.

PAULA: O.K. I'll wait. Take your time.

FEFU: It's going to take quite a while.

PAULA: It's all right. I'll wait.

FEFU: Do me a favor?

PAULA: Sure. Open up and I'll do you a favor.

(*There is the sound of a pot falling , a door slamming.*)

FEFU: Fill it up for me.

PAULA: O.K.

FEFU: Thank you.

PAULA: Here's water. Open up.

FEFU: Leave it there. I'll come out in a minute.

PAULA: O.K. Here it is. I'm leaving now.

(Loud steps. Paula comes down with a filled pan. Emma hides by the entrance to the steps. Emma splashes water on Paula. Paula splashes water on Emma. Sue appears with a full pan.)

PAULA: Truce!

SUE: Who's the winner?

PAULA: You are. You do the dishes.

SUE: I'm the winner. You do the dishes.

FEFU: *(From the landing.)* Line up!

SUE: Psst. *(Paula and Emma look. Sue splashes water on them.)* Gotcha!

EMMA: Please don't.

PAULA: Truce. Truce.

FEFU: O.K. Line up. *(Pointing to the kitchen.)* Get in there! *(They all go to the kitchen.)* Start doing those dishes. *(There is a moment's pause.)*

JULIA: It's over.

CINDY: We're safe.

JULIA: *(To Christina.)* You can come up now. *(Christina stays down.)* You rather wait a while. *(Christina nods.)*

CHRISTINA: *(Playful.)* I feel danger lurking.

CINDY: She's been hiding all day.

(Fefu enters. She is wet.)

FEFU: I won. I got them working.

JULIA: I thought the fight was over who'd do the dishes.

FEFU: Yes. *(Starting to go.)* I have to change. I'm soaked.

CHRISTINA: They forgot what the fight was about.

FEFU: We did?

JULIA: That's usually the way it is.

FEFU: (*Going to Christina and lifting the cover from her face.*) Are you ready for an ice cube?

(*Fefu exits upstairs. Christina runs upstairs. There is silence.*)

CINDY: So.—And how have you been?

JULIA: All right. I've been taking care of myself.

CINDY: You look well.

JULIA: I do not. . . . Have you seen Mike?

CINDY: No, not since Christmas.

JULIA: I'm sorry.

CINDY: I'm O.K.—And how's your love life?

JULIA: Far away. . . . I have no need for it.

CINDY: I'm sorry.

JULIA: Don't be. I'm very morbid these days. I think of death all the time.

PAULA: (*Standing in the doorway.*) Anyone for coffee? (*They raise their hands.*) Anyone take milk? (*They raise their hands.*)

JULIA: Should we go in?

PAULA: I'll bring it out. (*Paula exits.*)

JULIA: I feel we are constantly threatened by death, every second, every instant, it's there. And every moment something rescues us. Something rescues us from death every moment of our lives. For every moment we live we have to thank something. We have to be grateful to something that fights for us and saves us. I have felt lifeless and in the face of death. Death is not anything. It's being lifeless and I have felt lifeless sometimes for a brief moment, but I have been rescued by these . . . guardians. I am not sure who these guardians are. I only know they exist because I have felt their absence. I think we have come to know them as life, and we have become familiar with certain forms they take. Our sight is a form they take. That is why we take pleasure in seeing things, and we find some things beautiful. The sun is a guardian. Those things we take pleasure in are usually guardians. We enjoy looking at the sunlight when it comes through the window. Don't we? We, as people, are guardians to each other when we give love. And then of course we have white cells and antibodies protecting us. Those moments when I feel lifeless have occurred, and I am afraid one day the guardians won't come in time and I will be defenseless. I will die . . . for no apparent reason.

(*Pause. Paula stands in the doorway with a bottle of milk.*)

PAULA: (*In a low-keyed manner.*) Anyone take rotten milk? (*Pause.*) I'm kidding. This one is no good but there's more in there . . . (*Remaining in good spirits.*) Forget it. It's not a good joke.

JULIA: It's good.

PAULA: In there it seemed funny but here it isn't. (*As she exits and shrugging her shoulders.*) It's a kitchen joke. Bye.

JULIA: (*After her.*) It is funny, Paula. (*To Cindy.*) It was funny.

CINDY: It's all right, Paula doesn't mind.

JULIA: I'm sure she minds. I'll go see . . . (*Julia starts to go. Paula appears in the doorway.*)

PAULA: (*In a low-keyed manner.*) Hey, who was that lady I saw you with?—That was no lady. That was my rotten wife. That one wasn't good either, was it? (*Exiting.*) Emma. . . . That one was no good either.

(*Sue starts to enter carrying a tray with sugar, milk, and two cups of coffee. She stops at the doorway to look at Paula and Emma who are behind the wall.*)

SUE: (*Whispering.*) What are you doing?—What?—O.K., O.K. (*She enters whispering. Sue puts the tray down.*) They're plotting something.

(*Paula appears in the doorway.*)

PAULA: (*In a low-keyed manner.*) Ladies and gentlemen. Ladies, since our material is too shocking and avant-garde, we have decided to uplift our subject matter so it's more palatable to the sensitive public. (*Paula takes a pose. Emma enters. She lifts an imaginary camera to her face.*)

EMMA: Say cheese.

PAULA: Cheese. (*They both turn front and smile. The others applaud.*) Ah, success, success. Make it clean and you'll succeed.— Coffee's in the kitchen.

SUE: Oh, I brought theirs out.

PAULA: Oh, shall we have it here?

JULIA: We can all go in the kitchen. (*They each take their coffee and go to the kitchen. Sue takes the tray to the kitchen. The sugar remains on the table.*)

PAULA: Either here or there. (*She sits on the couch.*) I'm exhausted.

(*Cecilia enters from the lawn.*)

CECILIA: Is the war over?

PAULA: Yes.

CECILIA: It's nice out. (*Paula nods in agreement.*) Where's everybody?

PAULA: In the kitchen, having coffee.

CECILIA: We must talk. (*Paula starts to speak.*) Not now. I'll call you. (*Cecilia starts to go.*)

PAULA: When?

CECILIA: I don't know.

PAULA: I don't want you, you know.

CECILIA: I know.

PAULA: No, you don't. I'm not lusting after you.

CECILIA: I know that. (*She starts to go.*) I'll call you.

PAULA: When?

CECILIA: As soon as I can.

PAULA: I won't be home then.

CECILIA: When will you be home?

PAULA: I'll check my book and let you know.

CECILIA: Do that.—I'll be leaving after coffee. I'll say goodbye now.

PAULA: Goodbye. (*Cecilia goes towards the kitchen. Paula starts towards the steps. Fefu comes down the steps.*)

FEFU: You're still wet.

PAULA: I'm going to change now.

FEFU: Do you need anything?

PAULA: No, I have something I can change to. Thank you.

(*As Paula goes upstairs, Fefu comes down the steps. She is downcast. The lights shift to an eerie tone. Fefu hallucinates the following: Julia enters in slow motion, walking. She goes to the coffee table, gets the sugar bowl, lifts it in Fefu's direction, takes the cover off, puts it back on and walks to the kitchen. As soon as Julia exits, Sue's voice is heard speaking the following lines. Immediately after, Julia re-enters wheeled by Sue. Cindy, Christina, Emma, and Cecilia are with them. On the arms of the wheelchair rests a tray with a coffee pot and cups. As they reach the couch and chairs they sit. Sue puts the tray on the table. Fefu stares at Julia.*)

SUE: I was terribly exhausted and run down. I lived on coffee so I could stay up all night and do my work. And they used to give us these medical check-ups all the time. But all they did was ask how we felt and we'd say "Fine," and they'd check us out. In the meantime I looked like a ghost. I was all bones. Remember Susan Austin? She was very naive and when they asked her how she felt, she said she was nervous and she wasn't sleeping well. So she had to see a psychiatrist from then on.

EMMA: Well, she was crazy.

(*Fefu exits.*)

SUE: No, she wasn't.—Oh god, those were awful days. . . . Remember Julie Brooks?

EMMA: Sure.

SUE: She was a beautiful girl.

EMMA: Ah yes, she was gorgeous.

(*Paula comes down the stairs as soon as she has changed. She sits on the steps half way down.*)

SUE: At the end of the first semester they called her in because she had been out with 28 men and they thought that was awful. And the worst thing was that after that, she thought there was something wrong with her.

CINDY: (*Jokingly.*) She was a nymphomaniac, that's all.

SUE: She was not. She was just very beautiful so all the boys wanted to go out with her. And if a boy asked her to go have a cup of coffee she'd sign out and write in the name of the boy. None of us did of course. All she did was go for coffee or go to a movie. She was really very innocent.

EMMA: And Gloria Schuman? She wrote a psychology paper the faculty decided she didn't write and they called her in to try to make her admit she hadn't written it. She insisted she wrote it and they sent her to a psychiatrist also.

JULIA: Everybody ended going to the psychiatrist.

(*Fefu enters through the foyer.*)

EMMA: After a few visits the psychiatrist said: Don't you think you know me well enough now that you can tell me the truth about the paper? He almost drove her crazy. They just couldn't believe she was so smart.

SUE: Those were difficult times.

PAULA: We were young. That's why it was difficult. On my first year I thought you were all very happy. I had been so deprived in my childhood that I believed the rich were all happy. During the summer you spent your vacations in Europe or the Orient. I went to work and I resented that. But then I realized that many lives are ruined by poverty and many lives are ruined by wealth. I was always able to manage. And I think I enjoyed myself as much when I went to Revere Beach on my day off as you did when you visited the Taj Mahal. (*Cecilia enters from the foyer. She stands there and listens. Paula doesn't acknowledge her.*) Then, when I stopped feeling envy, I started noticing the waste. I began feeling contempt for those who, having everything a person can ask for, make such a mess of it. I resented them because they were not better than the poor. If you have all you need you should be generous. If you can afford to go to school your mind should be better. If you didn't have to fight for your place on earth you should be nobler. But I saw them cheating and grabbing like the kids in the slums, or wasting away with self-indulgence. And I saw them be plain stupid. If there is a reason why some are rich while others starve it must be so they put everything they have at the service of others. They should take the responsibility of everything that happens in the world. They are the only ones who can influence things. The poor don't have the power to change things. I think we should teach the poor and let the rich take care of themselves. I'm sorry, I know that's what we're doing. That's what Emma has been doing. I'm sorry . . . I guess I feel it's not enough. (*Paula sobs.*) I'll wash my face. I'll be right back. (*She starts to go towards the kitchen.*) I think highly of all of you. (*Cecilia follows her. Paula turns. Cecilia opens her arms and puts them around Paula, engulfing her. She kisses Paula on the lips. Paula steps back. She is fearful. Cecilia follows her. Fefu enters from the lawn.*)

FEFU: Have you been out? The sky is full of stars.

(*Emma, Sue, Christina, and Cindy exit.*)

JULIA: What's the matter?

(*Fefu shakes her head. Julia starts to go toward the door.*)

FEFU: Stay a moment, will you?

JULIA: Of course.

FEFU: Did you have enough coffee?

JULIA: Yes.

FEFU: Did you find the sugar?

JULIA: Yes. There was sugar in the kitchen. What's the matter?

FEFU: Can you walk? (*Julia is hurt. She opens her arms implying she hides nothing.*) I am sorry, my dear.

JULIA: What is the matter?

FEFU: I don't know, Julia. Every breath is painful for me. I don't know. (*Fefu turns Julia's head to look into her eyes.*) I think you know.

(*Julia breaks away from Fefu.*)

JULIA: (*Avoiding Fefu's glance.*) No, I don't know. I haven't seen much of you lately. I have thought of you a great deal. I always think of you. Cindy tells me how you are. I always ask her. How is Phillip? Things are not well with Phillip?

FEFU: No.

JULIA: What's wrong?

FEFU: A lot is wrong.

JULIA: He loves you.

FEFU: He can't stand me.

JULIA: He loves you.

FEFU: He's left me. His body is here but the rest is gone. I exhaust him. I torment him and I torment myself. I need him, Julia.

JULIA: I know you do.

FEFU: I need his touch. I need his kiss. I need the person he is. I can't give him up. (*She looks into Julia's eyes.*) I look into your eyes and I know what you see. (*Julia closes her eyes.*) It's death. (*Julia shakes her head.*) Fight!

JULIA: I can't.

FEFU: I saw you walking.

JULIA: No. I can't walk.

FEFU: You came for sugar, Julia. You came for sugar. Walk!

JULIA: You know I can't walk.

FEFU: Why not? Try! Get up! Stand up!

JULIA: What is wrong with you?

FEFU: You have given up!

JULIA: I get tired! I get exhausted! I am exhausted!

FEFU: What is it you see? (*Julia doesn't answer.*) What is it you see! Where is it you go that tires you so?

JULIA: I can't spend time with others! I get tired!

FEFU: What is it you see!

JULIA: You want to see it too?

FEFU: No, I don't. You're nuts, and willingly so.

JULIA: You know I'm not.

FEFU: And you're contagious. I'm going mad too.

JULIA: I try to keep away from you.

FEFU: Why?

JULIA: I might be harmful to you.

FEFU: Why?

JULIA: I am contagious. I can't be what I used to be.

FEFU: You have no courage.

JULIA: You're being cruel.

FEFU: I want to rest, Julia. How does a person rest. I want to put my mind at rest. I am frightened. (*Julia looks at Fefu.*) Don't look at me. (*She covers Julia's eyes with her hand.*) I lose my courage when you look at me.

JULIA: May no harm come to your head.

FEFU: Fight!

JULIA: May no harm come to your will.

FEFU: Fight, Julia!

(*Fefu starts shaking the wheelchair and pulling Julia off the wheelchair.*)

JULIA: I have no life left.

FEFU: Fight, Julia!

JULIA: May no harm come to your hands.

FEFU: I need you to fight.

JULIA: May no harm come to your eyes.

FEFU: Fight with me!

JULIA: May no harm come to your voice.

FEFU: Fight with me!

JULIA: May no harm come to your heart.

(*Christina enters. Fefu sees Christina, releases Julia. To Christina.*)

FEFU: Now I have done it. Haven't I. You think I'm a monster. (*She turns to Julia and speaks to her with kindness.*) Forgive me if you can. (*Julia nods.*)

JULIA: I forgive you.

(*Fefu gets the gun.*)

CHRISTINA: What in the world are you doing with that gun!

FEFU: I'm going to clean it!

CHRISTINA: I think you better not!

FEFU: You're silly!

(*Cecilia appears on the landing.*)

CHRISTINA: I don't care if you shoot yourself! I just don't like the mess you're making!

(*Fefu starts to go to the lawn and turns.*)

FEFU: I enjoy betting it won't be a real bullet! You want to bet!

CHRISTINA: No! (*Fefu exits. Christina goes to Julia.*) Are you all right?

JULIA: Yes.

CHRISTINA: Can I get you anything?

JULIA: Water. (*Cecilia goes to the liquor cabinet for water.*) Put some sugar in it. Could I have a damp cloth for my forehead? (*Christina goes toward the kitchen. Julia speaks front.*) I didn't tell her anything. Did I? I didn't.

CECILIA: (*Going to Julia with the water.*) About what?

JULIA: She knew.

(*There is the sound of a shot. Christina and Cecilia run out. Julia puts her hand to her forehead. Her hand goes down slowly. There is blood on her forehead. Her head falls back. Fefu enters holding a dead white rabbit.*)

FEFU: I killed it . . . I just shot . . . and killed it. . . . Julia . . .

(*Dropping the rabbit, Fefu walks to Julia and stands behind the chair as she looks at Julia. Sue and Cindy enter from the foyer, Emma and Paula from the kitchen, Christina and Cecilia from the lawn. They surround Julia. The lights fade.*)

Rebecca Schull as Fefu. (Photo: Rena Hansen)

Scene from New York Theater Strategy original production at Relativity Media Lab.
Left to right (seated): Connie Cicone, Margaret Harrington, Gordana Rashovich,
Gwendolyn Brown, Carolyn Hearn; (standing): Rebecca Schull, Joan Voukides,
Janet Biehl. (Photo: Rena Hansen)

ONE-SET VERSION OF
FEFU AND HER FRIENDS

In 1996, as the Baker Artist-in-Residence at Muhlenberg College, Allentown, Pennsylvania, Maria Irene Fornes adapted and directed her play in a one-set version. For this staging, the audience remained in place throughout the entire performance rather than breaking up into groups and moving to four different scenes in Part II. In directing the new version, nearly two decades after the original production, Fornes significantly shifted the order of scenes in Part II. Several new entrances and exits were added, and references in the scene on the lawn were changed from croquet to tennis. Fornes had always planned to create a simplified version of her play so that it could be done in theatres that did not have the spatial capacity of the initial conception.

The cast for the Muhlenberg Department of Theatre Arts production included Devon Allen (Fefu), Carey Kotula (Emma), Rebecca Levine (Cecilia), Megan McGlincy (Sue), Crystl Horton (Christina), Angelica Pinna-Perez (Paula), Monica Stufft (Cindy), and Eli Katz (Julia). Designers were Trui Malten (lighting), Michael Allen (set), and Michael McDonald (costumes).

Publication of the one-set version of *Fefu and Her Friends* is based on the preservation of the script and author's revisions during rehearsals by the actor and then Muhlenberg College faculty member, Devon Allen, who played Fefu in the production, and who subsequently directed it at Portland State University in 2011.

(Following blackout at the end of Part I, Part II begins.)

CHRISTINA: *(Practicing.)* Etes-vous externe ou demi-pension-naire? La cuisine de votre cantine est-elle bonne, passble ou mauvaise?

(She continues reading almost inaudibly. A moment passes.)

CINDY: *(Reading.)* A lady in Africa divorced her husband because he was a cheetah.

CHRISTINA: Oh, dear. *(They laugh. They go back to their reading. A moment passes.)* Est-ce que votre professeur interroge souvant les eleves?

(They go back to their reading. A moment passes.)

CINDY: I suppose . . . when a person is swept off their feet . . . the feet remain and the person goes off . . . with the broom.

CHRISTINA: No . . . when a person is swept off their feet . . . there is no broom.

CINDY: What does the sweeping?

CHRISTINA: An emotion . . . a feeling.

CINDY: Then emotions have bristles?

CHRISTINA: Yes.

CINDY: Now I understand. Do the feet remain?

CHRISTINA: No, the feet fly also . . . but separate from the body. At the end of the leap, just before the landing, they join the ankles and one is complete again.

CINDY: Oh, that sounds nice.

CHRISTINA: It is. Being swept off your feet is nice. Anything else?

CINDY: Not for now. (*They go back to their reading. A moment passes.*) Are you having a good time?

CHRISTINA: Yes, I'm very glad I came.

CINDY: Do you like everybody?

CHRISTINA: Yes.

CINDY: Do you like Fefu?

CHRISTINA: I do . . . She confuses me a little . . . I try to be honest . . . and I wonder if she is . . . I don't mean that she doesn't tell the truth. I know she does. I mean a kind of integrity. I know she has integrity too . . . But I don't know if she's careful with life . . . something bigger than the self . . . I suppose I don't mean with life but more with convention. I think she is an adventurer in a way. Her mind is adventurous. I don't know if there is dishonesty in that. But in adventure there is taking chances and risks, and then one has to, somehow, have less regard or respect for things as they are. That is, regard for a kind of convention, I suppose. I am probably ultimately a conformist, I think. And I suppose I do hold back for fear of being disrespectful or destroying something . . . and I admire those who are not. But I also feel they are dangerous to me. I don't think they are dangerous to the world; they are more useful than I am, more important, but I feel some of my life is endangered by their way of thinking. Do you understand?

CINDY: Yes, I do.

CHRISTINA: I guess I am proud and I don't like thinking that I am thoughtful of things that have no value. . . . I like her.

CINDY: I had a terrible dream last night.

CHRISTINA: What was it?

CINDY: I was at a dance. And there was a young doctor I had seen in connection with my health. We all danced in a circle and he

identified himself and said that he had spoken to Mike about
me, but that it was all right, that he had put it so that it was all
right. I was puzzled as to why Mike would mind and why he
had spoken to him. Then, suddenly everybody sat down on
the floor and pretended they were having singing lessons and
one person was practicing Italian. The singing professor was
being tested by two secret policemen. They were having him
correct the voice of someone they had brought. He apparently
didnt know how to do it. Then, one of the policemen put his
hands on his vocal cords and kicked him out the door. Then he
grabbed me and felt my throat from behind with his thumbs
while he rubbed my nipples with his pinkies. Then, he pushed
me out the door. Then, the young doctor started cursing me.
His mouth moved like the mouth of a horse. I was on an upper
level with a railing and I said to him, "Stop and listen to me."
I said it so strongly that he stopped. Everybody turned to me
in admiration because I had made him stop. Then, I said to
him, "Restrain yourself." I wanted to say respect me. I wasn't
sure whether the words coming out of my mouth were what I
wanted to say. I turned to ask my sister. The young man was
bending over and trembling in mad rage. Another man told
me to run before the young man tried to kill me. Meg and I
ran downstairs. She asked me if I wanted to go to her place. We
grabbed a taxi, but before the taxi got enough speed he came
out and ran to the taxi and was on the verge of opening the
door when I woke up.

(*Paula enters through French doors. She holds a notebook. She
goes to the door left, looks out, and sits on a chair, upstage of the
other women. A moment later Fefu enters from upstage.*)

FEFU: (*From kitchen in doorway center. She holds a racquet.*)
  Who's for tennis?

(*Christina raises her finger. Cindy does also.*)

FEFU: Come.

(They start to go out.)

FEFU: Paula?

PAULA: In a little while.

CINDY: (*As they exit.*) I'll watch.

FEFU: (*To Paula.*) Do come.

PAULA: I will.

(Fefu, Christina, and Cindy exit left through French doors. Paula goes to the couch and sits.)

FEFU: (*From off-stage.*) I'll get us some lemonade. I'll bring it out.

(Fefu enters through French doors moving to kitchen.)

FEFU: (*From the kitchen off-stage.*) Sue, come out and play. You're working too hard.

(Fefu, carrying lemonade, enters from kitchen and exits through French doors.)

SUE: (*From the kitchen.*) I will.

(Paula sits on the sofa cross-legged. She opens up the notebook and starts to write. She stops writing and thinks for a moment. Then, she starts writing again. Sue enters from the kitchen. She is wearing an apron. She sits on a chair upstage. Paula continues writing for a while.)

PAULA: I have it all figured out.

SUE: What?

PAULA: A love affair lasts seven years and three months.

SUE: It does?

PAULA: (*Reading.*) 3 months of love. 1 year saying: it's all right. This is just a passing disturbance. 1 year trying to understand what's wrong. 2 years knowing the end had come. 1 year finding they way to end it. After the separation, 2 years trying to understand what happened. 7 years, 2 months. (*No longer reading.*) At any point the sequence might be interrupted by another love affair that has the same sequence. That is, it's not really interrupted, the new love affair relegates the first one to a second plane and both continue their sequence at the same time.

(*Sue looks over Paula's shoulder.*)

SUE: You really added it up.

PAULA: Sure. The old love affair may fade, so you are not aware the process goes on. A year later it may surface and you might find yourself figuring out what's wrong with the new one while trying to end the old one.

SUE: So how do you solve the problem?

PAULA: Celibacy?

SUE: You think celibacy?

PAULA: Maybe not.

SUE: What do you want to drink?

PAULA: Water.

SUE: Water it'll be.

(*Sue goes to the kitchen. Paula writes. Sue re-enters with a tray of ice cubes with a popsicle stick in each cube.*)

What's this? Dessert?

(She takes another cube and moves her arms in a Judo style.)

Eskimo wrestling.

(She places one stick behind her ear.)

Brain cooler. That's when you're thinking too much. You could use one.

(She tries to put the ice cube behind Paula's ear. They wrestle and laugh. She puts the stick in her mouth. She takes it out to speak.)

This is when you want to keep chaste. No one will kiss you.

(She puts it back in to demonstrate. Then takes it out.)

That's good for celibacy. If you walk around with one of these in your mouth for seven years you can keep all your sequences straight. Finish one before you start the other.

EMMA: *(Applauding and entering from the kitchen.)* Good, good, very, very nice. Thank you, thank you.

(Sue puts the ice cube in the tray and looks at it.)

SUE: A frozen caterpillar.

(Emma applauds.)

EMMA: Very, very nice. Very, very, very, very, very good.

SUE: Thank you, thank you, thank you.

PAULA: You're leaving that ice cube in there?

SUE: I'm clean.

EMMA and SUE: Very, very good. Very, very, very, very good. Thank you, thank you, thank you, thank you, thank you.

(Sue and Emma go into the kitchen with their arms around each other. Paula writes. There are the sounds of the tennis racquets hitting the balls from the left. A while later Sue re-enters and sits down.)

SUE: So, what else do you have on love?

PAULA: Well, the break-up takes place in parts. The brain, the heart, the body, mutual things, shared things. The mind leaves but the heart is still there. The heart has left but the body wants to stay.

(There is a pause.)

(Christina and Fefu are strolling onto the patio.)

CHRISTINA: *(From off-stage.)* What kind of bird is that?

FEFU: It's a red finch.

CHRISTINA: What's it doing?

FEFU: It's looking for food.

CHRISTINA: What does it eat?

FEFU: Seeds and worms.

CHRISTINA: That's what they eat?

FEFU: Fruit, too.

(Fefu exits to tennis court.)

CHRISTINA: That's more sensible.

(Christina follows Fefu.)

(Emma enters from the kitchen and goes toward the French doors. She speaks out.)

EMMA: Fefu!

FEFU: (*From off-stage.*) Yes?

EMMA: I can't find the other racquets.

FEFU: (*Off-stage.*) Where's Cindy?

EMMA: She's in the kitchen.

FEFU: (*Off-stage.*) Ask her if she knows where the racquets are.

CINDY: (*From off-stage.*) I last saw them in the kitchen closet.

EMMA: They're not there.

FEFU: (*Off-stage.*) I'll go look for them.

EMMA: No, you start playing. I'll find them.

FEFU: (*Off-stage.*) Ok.

(*There are the sounds of the tennis racquets hitting the balls and scoring conversations from the left.*)

FEFU: (*Off-stage.*) You could've gotten that.

CHRISTINA: (*Off-stage.*) No, I couldn't.

FEFU: (*Off-stage.*) Yes, you could've.

EMMA: (*To herself as she starts to go to the kitchen.*) No, she couldn't.

(*The sounds from outside continue. A few moments later Emma is heard.*)

EMMA: (*From off-*stage.) Fefu!

FEFU: (*Off-stage.*) Yes . . .

EMMA: (*Off-stage.*) I found them.

FEFU: (*Off-stage.*) Where were they?

EMMA: (*Off-stage.*) In the closet in the kitchen.

FEFU: (*Off-stage.*) That's where I thought they were.

EMMA: That's where they were.

(*Pause.*)

  Can I play now?

FEFU: We're waiting for you.

(*Sue looks out the window. There are the sounds of a tennis game.*)

SUE: (*Walking towards Paula.*) So, what else do you have?

PAULA: (*Reading.*) The body leaves but the things are still at the apartment. You must come back. You move everything out of the apartment but the mind stays behind. Memory lingers in the place. Seven years later, perhaps seven years later, it doesn't matter anymore. Perhaps it takes longer. Perhaps it never ends.

SUE: . . . it depends.

PAULA: Yup. It depends.

SUE: Something's bothering you.

PAULA: No.

(*There is a pause.*)

SUE: I think there is.

(*Paula lowers her head. Sue goes to her. A moment passes.*)

I think the soup is done. I'm going to see if Julia wants some.

PAULA: Go ahead.

(*Sue exits. There is a pause.*)

CINDY: (From off-stage.) Are we playing a real game?

FEFU: (Off-stage.) Of course.

(*Paula continues writing. A few moments after Cecilia appears at the entrance left. During the following scene Cecilia maintains a cordial yet somewhat distant tone.*)

CECILIA: May I come in?

(*Paula nods.*)

PAULA: Sure.

CECILIA: I've been meaning to call you.

PAULA: It doesn't matter. I know you're busy.

CECILIA: Still I would have called you but I really didn't find the time.

PAULA: Don't worry.

CECILIA: I wanted to see you again. I want to see you often.

PAULA: There's no hurry. Now we know we can see each other.

CECILIA: Yes, I'm glad we can.

PAULA: I have thought a great deal about my life since I saw you. I have questioned my life. I can't help doing that. It's been many years and I wondered how you see me now.

CECILIA: You're the same.

PAULA: I felt small in your presence . . . I haven't done all that I could have. All I wanted to do. Our lives have gone in such different directions I cannot help but review what those years have been for me. I gave up, almost gave up. I have missed you in my life . . . I became lazy. I lost the drive. You abandoned me and I kept going. But after a while I didn't know how to. I didn't know how to go on. I knew why when I was with you. To give you pleasure. So we could laugh together. So we could rejoice together. To bring beauty to the world . . . Now we look at each other like strangers. I speak and you don't understand my words. I remember every day.

(*Cecilia steps toward Paula. There is a hold, and then Fefu is heard off-stage.*)

FEFU: (*From off-stage.*) Oh boy.

(*Fefu entering, while speaking, from patio, carrying empty pitcher.*)

Oh boy, oh boy, oh boy. I don't blame you for staying in. It's getting very hot outside. I'm getting some more lemonade. Would you like some?

CECILIA: No, thank you.

(*Fefu exits into kitchen. Fefu re-enters from kitchen. She holds a pitcher with lemonade and extra glasses.*)

FEFU: Get some later if you change your mind. I'll keep it in the cooler. Paula? Cecilia?

(*Fefu starts to exit to tennis court.*)

PAULA: Yes, I'll come with you.

(*Cecilia goes upstairs. Fefu and Paula exit through the French doors up left.*)

(Julia wheels herself in from the back. She starts on the chair, moves to the couch, and ends on the floor.)

JULIA: They clubbed me. They broke my head. They broke my will. They broke my hands. They tore my eyes out. They took my voice away. They didn't do anything to my heart because I didn't bring my heart with me. They clubbed me again, but my head did not fall off in pieces. That was because they were so good and they felt sorry for me. The judges. You didn't know the judges? . . . I was good and quiet. I never dropped my smile. I smiled to everyone. If I stopped smiling I would get clubbed because they love me. They say they love me. I go along with that because if I don't . . .

(With her finger she indicates her throat being cut and makes the sound that usually accompanies that gesture.)

I told them the stinking parts of the body are the important ones: the genitals, the anus, the mouth, the armpit. All important parts except the armpits. And who knows, maybe the armpits are important too. That's what I said.

(Her voice becomes gravelly and tight in imitation of the judges.)

He said that all those parts must be kept clean and put away. He said that women's entrails are heavier than anything on earth and to see a woman running creates a disparate and incongruous image in the mind. It's anti-aesthetic. Therefore women should not run. Instead they should strike positions that take into account the weight of their entrails. Only if they do, can they be aesthetic. He said, for example, Goya's Maja. He said Ruben's women are not aesthetic. Flesh. He said that a woman's bottom should be in a cushion, otherwise it's revolting. He said there are exceptions. Ballet dancers are exceptions. They can run and lift their legs because they have no entrails. Isadora Duncan had entrails, that's why she should not have danced. But she danced and for this reason became crazy. (Her voice is back to normal.) She wasn't crazy.

(*She moves her hand as if guarding from a blow.*)

She was. He said that I had to be punished because I was getting too smart. I'm not smart. I never was. Neither is Fefu smart. They are after her too. Well, she's still walking!

(*She guards from a blow. Her eyes close.*)

Wait! I'll say my prayers. I'm saying it.

(*She mumbles. She opens her eyes with caution.*)

You don't think I'm going to argue with them, do you? I repented. I told them exactly what they wanted to hear. They killed me. I was dead. The bullet didn't hit me. It hit the deer. But I died. He didn't. Then I repented and the deer died and I lived. (*With a gravelly voice.*) They said, "Live but crippled. And if you tell . . . ."

(*She repeats the throat cutting gesture.*)

Why do you have to kill Fefu, for she's only a joker? (*With a gravelly voice.*) "Not kill, cure. Cure her." Will it hurt?

(*She whimpers.*)

Oh, dear, dear, my dear, they want your light. Your light my dear. Your precious light. Oh dear, my dear.

(*Her head moves as if slapped.*)

Not cry. I'll say my prayer. I'll say it. Right now. Look.

(*She sits up as if pulled by an invisible force.*)

The human being is of the masculine gender. The human being is a boy as a child and grown up he is a man. Everything on earth is for the human being, which is man. To nourish him. — There are evil things on earth, and noxious things. Evil and noxious things are on earth for man also. For him to fight with, and conquer and turn its evil into good. So that it too can nourish him. — There are Evil Plants, Evil Animals, Evil Minerals, and Women are Evil. — Woman is not a human being. She is: 1 — A mystery. 2 — Another species. 3 — As yet undefined. 4 — Unpredictable; therefore wicked and gentle and evil and good which is evil. — If a man commits an evil act, he must be pitied. The evil comes from outside him, through him and into the act. Woman generates the evil herself. — God gave man no other mate but woman. The oxen is good but it is not a mate for man. The sheep is good but it is not a mate for man. The mate for man is woman and that is the cross man must bear. — Man is not spiritually sexual, he therefore can enjoy sexuality. His sexuality is physical which means his spirit is pure. Women's spirit is sexual. That is why after coitus they dwell in nefarious feelings. Because that is their natural habitat. That is why it is difficult for them to return with them til they die. And they take those feelings with them to the afterlife where they corrupt the heavens, and they are sent to hell where through suffering they may shed those feelings and return to earth as man.

(*Her head moves as if slapped.*)

Don't hit me. Didn't I just say my prayer?

(*A smaller slap.*)

I believe it.

(*She lies back.*)

They say when I believe the prayer I will forget the judges. And when I forget the judges I will believe the prayer. They say both happen at once. And all women have done it. Why can't I? Fefu, watch out. They're after you.

(*At the end of Julia's speech, Fefu finds her.*) (*Blackout.*)

(*In blackout, Fefu exits off stage left. Julia exits. Lights. Emma enters from kitchen with small crate of root vegetables. Fefu starts speaking from off. She enters with straw hat, smock and box. They are moving small wooden crates from the kitchen to the cellar of stage left.*)

EMMA: (*Re-enters carrying a box as Fefu exits.*) Do you think about genitals all the time?

FEFU: Genitals? No, I don't think about genitals all the time.

EMMA: (*Starting to exit.*) I do, and it drives me crazy. Each person I see in the street, anywhere at all . . . I keep thinking of their genitals, what they look like, what position they are in. I think it's odd that everyone has them. Don't you?

FEFU: (*Crossing Emma.*) No, I think it'd be odder if they didn't have them.

(*Emma laughs.*) (*Fefu re-enters.*)

EMMA: I mean, people act as if they don't have genitals.

FEFU: How do people with genitals act?

EMMA: I mean, how can business men and women stand in a room and discuss business without even one reference to their genitals. I mean everybody has them. They just pretend they don't.

FEFU: I see. (*Shifting her glance from left to right with a fiendish look.*) You mean they should do this all the time.

(*Emma laughs.*)

EMMA: No, I don't mean that. Think of it. Don't you think I'm right?

FEFU: Yes, I think you're right. (*Fefu sits.*) Oh, Emma, Emma, Emma Emma.

EMMA: That's m'name. .... Well, you see, it's generally believed that you go to heaven if you are good. If you are bad you go to hell. That is correct. However, in heaven they don't judge goodness they way we think. They don't? They have a divine registry of sexual performance. In that registry they mark down every little sexual activity in your life. If your faith is not entirely in it, if you just perform as an obligation and you don't feel the most profound devotion, if your spirit, your heart, and your flesh is not religiously delivered to it, you are condemned. They put you down in the black list and you don't go to heaven. Heaven is populated with divine lovers. And in hell live the duds.

FEFU: That's probably true.

EMMA: I knew you'd see it that way.

FEFU: Oh, I do. I do. You see, on earth we are judged by public acts, and sex is a private act. The partner cannot be said to be the public, since both partners are engaged. So naturally, it stands to reason that it's angels who judge our sexual life.

EMMA: Naturally.

(*Pause.*)

FEFU: You always bring joy to me.

EMMA: Thank you.

FEFU: I thank you. (*Fefu becomes distressed. She sits.*) I am in constant pain. I don't want to give in to it. If I do I am afraid I will never recover ... It's not physical, and its not sorrow. It's very strange Emma, I can't describe it, and it's very frighten-ing ... It is as if normally there is a lubricant ... not in the body ... a spiritual lubricant ... it's hard to describe ... and without it, life is a nightmare, and everything is distorted. —A black cat started coming to my kitchen. He's awfully mangled and big. He is missing an eye and his skin is diseased. At first I was repelled by him, but then, I thought, this is a monster that has been sent to me and I must feed him. And I fed him. One day he came and shat all over my kitchen. Foul Diarrhea. He still comes and I still fed him. —I am afraid of him. How about a little lemonade?

EMMA: Yes.

(*Fefu exits. Emma improvises an effigy of Fefu. She puts Fefu's hat and gloves on it.*)

> Not from the stars do I my judgment pluck.
> And yet methinks I have astronomy;
> But not to tell of good or evil luck,
> Of plagues, of dearths, or seasons' quality;
> Nor can I fortune to brief minutes tell,
> Pointing to each his thunder, rain, and wind,
> Or say with princes if it shall go well
> By oft predict that I in heaven find.
> But from thine eyes my knowledge I derive.
> And, constant stars, in them I read such art
> As truth and beauty shall together thrive
> If from thyself to store thou wouldst convert:
>   Or else of thee this I prognosticate,
>   Thy end is truth's and beauty's doom and date.

(*Light fades to black. Intermission.*) (*After Intermission, the play continues with Part III.*)

INTERVIEW WITH MARIA IRENE FORNES

This interview with Maria Irene Fornes was taped in November 1977, by Bonnie Marranca, then Literary Advisor of the American Place Theatre. Fornes directed the production of her play there, which ran from January 8 to February 5, 1978.

> Fefu and Her Friends *is a departure from your other plays, which are non-realistic, isn't it?*

My first work on the play actually was less realistic. The play started in 1964. That is when I wrote some of the first scene, when Fefu takes a gun and shoots at her husband out the window .... Whether the play is realistic or less realistic has to do with the distance I have from it. I feel that the characters of *Fefu* are standing around me while other plays I see more at a distance. When I view a play far away from me, perhaps the characters become two-dimensional. They become more like drawings than flesh and blood. The question of what ends up being a realistic play has to do with the fact that one can feel the characters breathe, rather than in a more abstract play where it is the play that breathes, not the characters.

> *Do you feel that each of* the *eight women is symbolic or representative of a female personality type or quality?*

I don't think so at all. Doesn't every character in every play have a different character than the next one? The fact that *Fefu* is plotless might contribute to the feeling that if the women are not related to each other, and not related to the plot, then perhaps they represent certain types. In a plot play the woman is either the mother or the sister or the girlfriend or the daughter. The purpose of the character is to serve a plot so the relationship is responding to the needs of the plot. Although *Fefu* is realistic, the relationship of the women, in that sense, is abstract. The purposes these characters are serving is different from how a character serves a plot.

How are you distinguishing between plot and plotless plays?

Plot, which has generally been the basis for plays, deals with the mechanics of life in a practical sense, with the mechanics of the peculiar arrangement a society makes. For example, a plot story in Alaska might be that in winter there was more sun than usual, the protagonist is in deep distress and commits suicide. And we would say: Why is that a reason for distress? Then we find out that there is reason for distress when there is more sun because the fish don't swim close to the surface. Therefore, there is no food and there is a reason for famine. There is a reason for unhappiness, a reason to commit suicide. So that in dealing with plot we are dealing with those things that have to do with external life—the mechanics of how we manage in the world. A plotless play doesn't deal with the mechanics of the practical arrangement of life but deals with the mechanics of the mind, some kind of spiritual survival, a process of thought.

Fefu is a fascinating woman. She seems to be the center of the play, the most complex woman in it. Did the idea of the play grow out of the idea of Fefu?

Fefu took over the play . . . She is the woman in the first scene that I wrote, the woman who shoots her husband as a game. The source of this play is a Mexican joke: There are two Mexicans in sombreros sitting at a bullfight and one says to the other, "Isn't she beautiful, the one in yellow?" and he points to a woman on the other side of the arena crowded with people. The other one says, "Which one?" and he takes his gun and shoots her and says, "The one that falls." In the first draft of the play Fefu explains that she started playing this game with her husband because of that joke. But in rewriting the play I took out this explanation. The woman who plays such a game with her husband grabbed me. Fefu is complex, but I find her a very unified person. However, by conventional terms she is contradictory, she is very outrageous. Fefu is very close to me, so I tend to understand her and find her not unusual at all . . . I said that Fefu took over the play but it's not really so. Julia is an important voice and there are times when I feel the whole play is her. Although Fefu has more of a mind than Julia, Julia is the mind of the play—the seer, the visionary.

You first began the play in 1964. When did you begin working on it again?

About five years ago, in 1972. I did a considerable amount of work then during an intensive period of two or three months. When I stopped working on it—for whatever reason—I put it away and didn't think about it again. At the beginning of 1977 I decided that I would do a play for the Theatre Strategy season. Each year I would think of doing a play, then I would become so involved in administration and not do it. I got a date to do a play but I wasn't sure which one I would do because I had another play that I was very interested in, and there were possibilities of other things I had started. I decided since I had so little time I would read what I had written of these various plays and whichever one would grab me the most I would work on. When I looked at *Fefu* my feeling toward it was so intense that I knew that was the one I should work on.

In the last several years it has usually been experimental theatre directors rather than playwrights who have worked with environmental theatre concepts. Yet you have structured Fefu *around five different environments. How did the environmental concept evolve?*

When I had a date for the play to be performed I had to start looking for a place to perform it. I saw this place, the Relativity Media Lab on lower Broadway, and looked at the main performing area and thought it wasn't right. But I liked the place and the general atmosphere very much. The people who owned the place took me to different parts of the loft and said, "This room could be used for a dressing room," and I thought this room is so nice it could be used for a room in Fefu's house. They took me to another room and said, "This you can use as a green room," and I thought this is nice, this could be a room in Fefu's house. They took me to the office where we were to discuss terms, dates, etc. I thought this could be a room in Fefu's house. Then right there I thought I would like to do the play using these different rooms . . . So then I went home and continued writing the play with this new concept in mind.

> *Experiencing the play, moving from room to room, becomes more important than following a story. When you watch something in a conventional proscenium setting you have a fixed perspective. Whereas here you are in the actual rooms, moving about a house.*

I think what makes it special is the fact that there are four walls. If the audience went inside a set that had only three walls, there would be a sense that this is not a room but a set. The fact that in *Fefu* you are enclosed inside the rooms with the actors is really the difference. You are aware of the four walls around you, and it is very important that the audience be on only two sides of the room. So when you look at the actors you should not see the audience behind them. Perhaps it's more a question of being a witness than . . .

> *an average spectator. You're not really following a story or plot but are overhearing conversations in a way, witnessing a series of encounters. The audience is involved in the play in a much more experiential way than is common.*

I expected that the audience would feel as if they are really visiting people in their house.

> *In some ways Fefu seems Chekhovian—a kind of mood piece. Do you think so?*

I think so, even though I didn't think of Chekhov when I wrote it. I don't know if one could analyze it technically and find similarities. What would be similarities?—the way dialogue proceeds, the presentation of a section of an event. I haven't studied Chekhov. But I think in spirit it is very Chekhovian, and also, though it is realistic, *Fefu* is very abstract, as Chekhov is.

Is it a feminist play? Fefu shows women together on stage as they have rarely been seen before.

Is it a feminist play?

Fefu is not a militant or ideological play, but by feminist I mean it has all women characters who do not relate to one another in terms of stereotypes. They have a certain way of being in the world, a certain perspective that is seen from the female eye.

Yes, it is a feminist play. The play is about women. It's a play that deals with each one of these women with enormous tenderness and affection. I have not deliberately attempted to see these women "as women have rarely been seen before." I show the women as I see them and if it is different from the way they've been seen before, it's because that's how I see them. The play is not fighting anything, not negating anything. My intention has not been to confront anything. I felt as I wrote the play that I was surrounded by friends. I felt very happy to have such good and interesting friends.

There is a contemporary perspective in the characters. Yet, the play is set in 1935. Why?

The women were created in a certain way because of an affection I have for a kind of world which I feel is closer to the thirties than any other period. Simply because it is pre-Freud, in the way that people manifested themselves with each other there was something more wholesome and trusting, in a sense. People accepted each other at face value. They were not constantly interpreting each other or themselves. Before Freud became popular and infiltrated our social and emotional lives, if a person said, "I love so-and-so," the person listening would believe the statement. Today, there is an automatic disbelieving of everything that is said, and an interpreting of it. It's implied that there's always some kind of self-deception about an emotion.

*You speak about wholesomeness in the characters in the play,
the acceptance of things at face value. What qualities were
you looking for when you cast the play?*

That very quality—wholesomeness. It has to do with not being
bitter, with accepting responsibility for what happens to you in
life. When I was casting it was very clear to me when a person
entered the room whether she belonged in the world of *Fefu*.

You also staged Fefu. *How do you like directing your own
work? Do you feel you can maintain a certain objectivity
about the text?*

I think so. You mentioned before that it is usually directors who
deal with environmental work rather than playwrights, and my
first thought was that I probably first responded to the loft environment that I visited as a director. However, since I am both
a director and a playwright it's difficult to separate the process
of creativity which, in me, has no separation. It isn't that I first
write the play and then direct it, like two different people. It's
a similar process that continues. However, when I'm writing a
play I'm planning what I am going to do when I direct it.

For me one of the great pleasures of Fefu *has to do with your
choice of a "natural," almost effortless performance style.
What were you attempting in the direction of the play?*

In the process of auditioning there were people who read for me
who were extremely talented but I thought they would shatter
the play. I began to see the play almost as if it had glass walls and
I felt there were people who would break the walls. A lot has
been said about the style of acting and the style of production
in *Fefu*, and that surprised me. I told the actors that the style of
acting should be film acting. That's how I saw it. Perhaps when
you do film acting on stage it seems very special. Do you think
it's any different from film acting?

The style of the production seems to be a kind of untheatrical naturalism—a certain flatness that appears stylized, very casual. As in film, the characters are seen in close-up, which is a big change from the way one relates to a theatre performance. Realistic plays are normally done from a fixed perspective. In Fefu, *not only is the style of acting cinematic, the structure of the play is cinematic, too. It incorporates jump cuts when you move from a study to a bedroom to a lawn. You don't get the beginning or end of a scene because you are going in and out of the different performing spaces.*

Pinter is done somewhat in this style of acting, isn't he? The timing in *Fefu* is very important. So is the texture of sound. For example, in the third scene—it moves back to the living room—if the timing is not impeccable there will be no scene. If someone else were to direct the play I think it would be very difficult to do unless it were thought of as music. For example, when the women are having a water fight there is a lot of laughter, a lot of screaming. In the scene that follows Julia talks about death. For that scene to begin, the sound of the laughter in the room has to have subsided completely. The laughter is like a substance that takes over the whole house, a laughter that comes from the kitchen to the living room almost like a body that moved around the house, then finally went back to the kitchen and subsided. And then, from total silence Cindy asks Julia a question and she begins talking about death. In *Fefu*, the style of writing in the first and third scenes is different from the style of writing in the close-up scenes in the center of the play. These scenes have a more theatrical style of writing, and though I also try to tone down the performances in them, they take on a larger life.

Fefu has many of the qualities of your other plays—whimsy, lightness of touch, economy of style, bittersweetness, an interest in exploring human relations. Yet it is also very different in that the characters, being realistic, are less given to dreams, myth or ritual. How do you view Fefu *in relation to your other work?*

I think *Fefu* comes straight from *Cap-a-Pie* because that play was based on the personal experiences and dreams and thoughts of the cast. Dealing so intimately with the realistic material left me with a desire to continue working in that manner. In *Aurora* there was a sense of characters going from one room to another though the scenes were not played simultaneously. I was not aware that this was happening in *Fefu* as it happened in *Aurora* until the day when I first rehearsed all the scenes together. I really don't see much difference between *Fefu* and my other plays. Any difference is a stylistic one. I think that tenderness toward the characters is what is at the core of my work and that is no different in *Fefu* than in the other plays.

Does Fefu *tell us where your future interests in drama lie?*

Perhaps it does. However, a great many people have found *Fefu* to be my most important work, and in doing so I feel that there is a subtle denial of my other plays. I like *Fefu* very, very much but I feel almost like a mother who's had eight children and the ninth is called the beautiful one, the intelligent one, and everybody is saying, "Aren't you glad you had this one?" You feel they are all your children. It could very well be that *Fefu* is more successful than my other plays and that it would be a clever thing for me to continue writing in this manner. I will if that is my inclination but not because I feel I have been on the wrong track previously. I don't see my work in relation to its possible impact in the world of theatre or the history of theatre. The shape that a play of mine takes has to do with my own need for a certain creative output.

CPSIA information can be obtained
at www.ICGtesting.com
Printed in the USA
JSHW052045200222
23131JS00004B/8

9 781555 541637